Praise for *When Snow Walks In*:

Christine's work is compelling. She takes us where she goes, down a street or to an art exhibit. Her work is a master of delights, each poem with a different view of small things. What color is that? You might ask. Never mind. The next moment the silver sky will be red like the horizon. She does not promise. Christine shows her moment and wants the readers to have their own.

— Annette Robinson

Christine Candland's first book of poems: *When Snow Walks In*, follows her two novels, *Topaz Woman* and *Pleiades Rising*, which were each awarded first prize, takes us on a journey through life and travels. Candland says, "I wanted to experience life but not be hurt by it." Through her poems, we are led on an experience of discovering intricate angles as she shows us, "Chess players take note of such things." Reading her experiences, we are enriched by this slim volume of an artist whose vision projects through various color prisms.

— Gedda Ilves

As I read the poetry of Christine Candland, I am fully there. Christine is a true student of the art of writing, having mastered the high realm of in-seeing and craft. Her skill with detail is the reader's portal into worlds of the commonplace and many of her stanzas stun me in their beauty:

> *Songs of drought and madness are carried by the soft wind*
> *while thunderbirds weep*
> *over uncarved destinies*
> *and sleepless sprites idle in the four o'clock sun.*

Thank you, Christine, for allowing me to participate. I can hear the slow tap of your poems.

— Gail Gauldin Moore

WHEN

SNOW

WALKS

IN

Christine Candland has written the following novels:

Topaz Woman

Cassidy Brookes discovers a rare Imperial Topaz brooch at an antiques fair and travels to Ouro Preto, a fabled city in Brazil known for its rivers of gold and emerald mines, in search of its legendary owner.

Pleiades Rising

When Maggie Marland and her friend Will Brighton discover a mysterious gold coin in an Indian cave in Malibu, their quest takes them to the pyramids of Mexico and the mysterious object that awaits them.

WHEN

SNOW

WALKS

IN

Poems By

CHRISTINE
CANDLAND

WHEN SNOW WALKS IN

Book designed and Edited by Michael N. Candland

iUniverse books may be ordered through booksellers or by contacting:

iUniverse
1663 Liberty Drive
Bloomington, IN 47403
www.iuniverse.com
844-349-9409

ISBN: 978-1-6632-0174-4 (sc)
ISBN: 978-1-6632-0176-8 (hc)
ISBN: 978-1-6632-0175-1 (e)

Library of Congress Control Number: 2020914807

Print information available on the last page.

iUniverse rev. date: 10/23/2020

Dedicated to my writer friends

who had the courage to pick up a pencil

and face a blank page in the first place.

Acknowledgments

Thank you to Beyond Baroque and the writers in my workshops whose wisdom and talent continue to inspire me.

Annette Robinson

Gedda Ilves

Gail Gauldin Moore

Vickie Riggs

Greg Moore

Sher McKinzi

Clare Chu

Anna Alra DerSarkisian

Alex Frankel

Raven Kras

Suzanne Weisberg

Howard Weisberg

Mark Fulton

Contents

THREE

ONE

Growing Too Tall

There was the time
when I was level with
knees,
grown-ups smiled and bent down.

There was the time I was
level with the boys in the
class when my eyes met
theirs and they smiled at me.

There was the time when
I grew beyond them,
when I saw the tops of
their heads,
had to search for their
eyes, which settled on
my chest.

That was the time

they stopped smiling

when they looked up

and wondered how

they could ever dance with me.

My Dad's Typewriter

It was an old Underwood upright.
They were still selling them in the '70s,
I think.

Letters to cousin Bud and promises to write,
still stuck to the platen.
An off-white enamel with black keys.

Don't touch it, interrupts my thoughts.

*But what can I use to type my stories on,
no one hears my voice.*

Now it sits on the back porch in the
rain.
He is gone and
no one knows what
to do with that old Underwood.

No one knows how to finish the letters

to cousin Bud

or how to unstick the promises to write,

why would they

he guarded it so well.

Don't touch it, got in the way.

One day it was thrown out.

No one remembers, why

should they?

I learned to write my own stories by hand,

saving them for another typewriter.

One that had sense enough

to stay out of the rain.

Trailing the Light

Seven a.m. yoga means getting up at six.
Translucent moon on the edge of morning as
streaks of red cross the eastern sky.

Heading south on Sepulveda, shadows hug buildings.
Cars in opposite lane
form a long searchlight.

Forgot my grocery list.

Need flour for bird's nest cookies,
and raspberry jam.

Our cocoon is a church gym.
Filtered light from the window
pours into the dark room.

Flow through your Vinyasa.

We snake our spines forward into a sphinx pose.

Find your Down Dog.

Lift our frame, form an arch.

Forgot to mail Sandy's letter.

Balance on one leg in Tree pose.

Lift your arms. Let your branches grow taller.

The line is so long at the post office.

Prepare for Sarvasana.

What was the name of that book?

Namaste.

Pencils

Pencils are my connector
to the page

from Palomino Blackwing Pearl
with brass crown and
obsidian lines of fine coal

to Dixon Ticonderoga,
a steady workhorse, yellow with green bands
medium lead

the feel of them in my hand
long and slick.

Do they prefer to be sharpened
all at once
or one at a time as I
proceed with purpose and resolve.

Gertrude Stein said *just get it down*
but I resist
suppose she was wrong.

Do they talk to each other
between hours
as they lie side by side
in the dreaded pencil box.

Taken out only when my muse
appears,
as she steps lightly toward me.

Are they on alert for the moment when they can
return to paper, lined or unlined

to finish a thought, capture a dream
unite words or notes for a song

which shall it be,
the Blackwing Pearl
or the Dixon Ticonderoga?

Riding High

I'm perched on the side of a mountain,
sitting in my 1964 Comet.
Waiting for the light to change.

How did I get here?

The day started out so well.
Shopping on Union Street,
bought a new belt and corduroy suit.
Blintzes at the Deli.

Thought I'd take a shortcut up Gough,
not the usual route.

Crossing Green, no problem.
Then Vallejo. Both green lights.
Okay, so far.

Then quickly I'm elevated.
Like climbing up the side of an elephant.

Then a yellow light on Broadway.
Vaulting up another hill.
Pacific is next. My street.
My heart soars—if I can just make it!

No, the light changes to red.
I pull out the emergency brake.
Breathing hard.
How could this have happened?
Everything was going so well.

Still perched on the side of the mountain.
Knuckles are white, against the red steering wheel.
One foot on the clutch, the other on the brake.
Knees knocking together.
Too many things to do at once.

I look in my rearview mirror.
A car is approaching from behind.
Doesn't he know I'm about to roll back any minute?
The light finally changes.

I rev up the engine.

Smoke billows out the back end.

Slowly, I let the clutch out.

The car inches forward.

The guy behind honks impatiently.

My hands are shaking.

I release the brake.

Pray the engine doesn't stall.

The car finally creeps forward,

onto the flat ground.

Safe at last.

Looking back, that was sort of fun.

Maybe I'll try it again, sometime.

Maybe.

Faces

I never knew faces
before going to art school,
not as architectural wonders.

Only as blank slates with cautious smiles
or laugh lines recognizable as friends or relatives.

Not as landscapes with destinations and mirrors
where cheekbones reflected charted boundaries
and foreheads spoke to structured confluence.

I never knew how to capture the soft pattern
of buttered skin with the ease of a graphite stroke.
Never recognized stern profiles resilient
to nocturnal lullabies.

Or how to calibrate a life lived by following
the slant of an eyebrow
or felt the weight of heavy-lidded eyes
as they beckoned me into
narrow portals and hidden corridors.

I learned there is no true symmetry.

Each side of a face is designed

independently.

A separate composition.

Our inclination to create balance must give way

to nature's harmony before interpreting the Rorschach

as it overlaps into one stilted gaze.

Sketching from memory takes us

to heightened experience.

Botticelli driven by passion

sketched page after page.

Until he recreated Simonetta

ten years after she died

as Aphrodite in *The Birth of Venus*.

Lucca

I fill my water bottle
from the town fountain
wondering if a hundred years of bottle filling

catches the same water next to the same river
next to the same hotel.

Hold on to the rail!
Shower floors are slippery.
Seamless like Carrara marble,
chosen by Michelangelo
to sculpt the *David*.

I reach for a triangle-shaped apple
from a brass bowl placed next
to the elevator.

Remember floor zero is really
floor one.

Walks on top of Roman walls
passing tulip trees, pink blossoms
cannon balls lying in aqueducts dry,
while stone lions guard the city
from Florentine invaders.

Puccini arias echo
throughout the Baptistery,
metal chairs squeak softly,
recipes for *chianina ragu* are sold
Saint Mary promises grace from a pedestal.

When, "watch out for the car" is heard
tourists scatter along the narrow street,
next to a wall-sized poster advertising
Elton John's last concert.

A postcard to be sent,
still in my pocket.

Before Daybreak

Somewhere between dawn and mischief
after turning on the heat

a roar of endless apologies
sinks down into the carpet.

Ginger with large yellow paws
is asleep,
traveling through landscapes
only she remembers.

The kettle is on,
hot water to make
that first cup of coffee.

Next door, the neighbors
are quiet.
We don't speak to them.
We don't know why anymore.

Somewhere, sanity lives
but only before daybreak, that's
for sure.

And time travel doesn't work
without a road map.

Desert Paint

She paints beside the adobe Abiquiu,
carefully arranging bleached
collarbones next to the spiny cactus,

which still has a life.

Squeezes the tube of zinc white
across the seaboard.

Watch me, the little girl calls out.

When no one answers, dolphin gray water
morphs into cobalt rivers.

Musty in that old attic.
Still searching for clues between
sheets of onion skin and rag rugs
twisted from worn rayon dresses.

A peppermint starlight
falls on the ground.

She bends down to pick it up,
just a drop of paint after all.

Songs of drought and madness are carried by
the soft wind while thunderbirds weep
over uncarved destinies,

and sleepless sprites idle
in the four o'clock sun.

Blue Stones

Wired to a leather bracelet tooled with
petroglyph images

last seen in a cave
south of Durango,
where the dragons live.

These stones unpolished are
stitched in harmonious rows
by wizards
who mix sentimental alchemy.

I've finished the last of the chocolate grahams
railing against words that fail to surface.
The bracelet is too large for my wrist,
as it shifts back and forth, restless.

When will the blue stones sing the songs
(I once knew but have since forgotten)

so I can gather them into a buckskin sack

to carry across the mountain pass

that closes during snowstorms, warning everyone

at the first sign of flurries.

Settling between the bones of my fingers,

I capture the melodic tones

trapped between octaves

finding the right vibration

that pulls it all together

once again.

Nellie, My Neighbor

Time is the well-placed adversary
nipping at my heels, the punches well intended.
Don't tarry too long, so the warning goes.

Don't replay memories of Nellie and I
knitting on Wednesdays.
Reminded of how clumsy my mind
could get over numbers of rows and
the size of needles.

But I look back, anyway.
The stucco house is still down the street
where Gunther's ear was torn off (almost)
the night she let him out thinking
she was doing him a favor.

I'll dally a few more moments

over Nellie's determination to get her hair
permed every three months,
all 95 years of her,
pushing back whenever anyone gave
her an impatient stare.

She meted her stories out shrewdly
making sure we all had one
to take home, to retell.

I wasn't around to catch her
when she fell
I had listened to time admonishing me for
sticking around too long as it was,

for watching through its window
thinking daylight wouldn't notice.

For getting too close to
the air conditioner that poured cold air down on my head

as I sat in the chair that rocked badly,
next to her bed with its myriad collection of pills
and a romance novel.
Not worth complaining about at the time
but scratches on the furniture I couldn't erase,
nevertheless.

Crystal Ponies

She talked to the crystal ponies for as long
as she could remember.
Moving them back and forth, in and out
of the roundabout

explaining the shadow they saw
didn't belong to the moon
but to its first cousin who lived on the mountain peak that
rested somewhere between indigo and pitch.

Noting it was the gingerbread gate that kept out the
snapshots of everyday life.

So they couldn't see where they lived.
So they couldn't run away.

One day, the ponies left on their own, anyway,
crossing the valley without her. The wrinkles
in their plumed headdresses had to be ironed
and their coats brushed for the next performance.

No one could blame them,
the circus doesn't wait.

She looked around for something else
to hold up her bones
but they melted away so fast she was caught off guard
and didn't have time to find a replacement.

She would have gone with them, she reasoned
but there were things that had to be done,
teacups to be dusted and felt pockets
to be sewn on the jackets.

Someone else would come along, sometime.
Sometime.

Celery

When Mom and Dad
talked about his salary
I thought they meant celery

and I dreamed of the stalks
being traded for dollars and

wondered if they weighed the celery whole
or just counted the stalks one by one.

When we were broke,
they would
fill the dented thermos

with coffee and make sandwiches,
bologna or ham, I can't remember

and they would drive down to the gas station
at the end of the block,
and sell them to the truckers who stopped
for gas.

I could tell when they came
home whether they had sold
anything or not

by the smile or not
on their faces.

They'd pull out the
change from their
pockets
sit down at the kitchen table
and count it.

How much they made meant
how well we'd eat until pay day.

Serendipity

Those years in San Francisco,
highlighted by paradox and second sight.

A girl last remembered, was it high school?
Recognizing me from a block away.

Our names escape us, but we know who we are.
"I always admired you," I say.
Her green eyes flash in appreciation.
She with polished scalloped nails,
me, wrapped in weathered wool.

"My life has been an unhappy one," she begins,
ending with an homage to her surgeon husband.

I separate lumps of clam from potatoes in my
chowder, as the front door of the café
swings open dousing us with rainy wind.

Ensconced somewhere on Knob Hill,
Brianna's world remains lofty.

I unwrap the cellophane from a saltine

cracker, which crumbles around the edges.

The red tie separates the two halves.

Salt grains fall on the table and in my lap.

Her eyes glaze over, as she recalls

trips to Paris, cruises to Venice,

social dinners; a deep sigh.

I ramble on, a single girl, kicking around in the city.

My studio apartment, three flights up

without an elevator,

steam heaters that hiss their news of the day.

Pots of fuchsias nurtured on the fire escape.

Despite promises made to keep in touch,

I never see her again.

TWO

Forgotten

The door opened and closed
the floorboards squeaked

and told stories that
held the house together for years.

The door opened again,
she didn't get out

but stayed inside and became
part of the woodwork and
the floors that squeaked.

Outside the window
the cottonwoods sang to the muses

who sat on the large boulder
invisible to everyone
but the most curious.

Years passed,

she must become herself.

Must separate from the wainscoting.

Trust that the muses

and the cottonwoods

would teach her to

sing a song for

herself.

She only had to ask.

The Ladies in the Neighborhood

When the ladies in the neighborhood wanted
someone to run an errand
I was there

to run down to the corner store
Wise potato chips were fifteen cents
Wonder bread was twenty cents

a carton of cigarettes was a dollar fifty,
my tip ranged from a dime to a quarter.

I savored the power of earning my own money.

When the ladies in the neighborhood
gave each other permanents
I was there

watching as they wrapped strands of
hair up in plastic rollers,
mixing the Toni formula

finishing off with neutralizer.
The smell of ammonia permeated
the air.

When the ladies in the neighborhood
visited each other,
I watched as they sipped their Cokes
and drew on Kool cigarettes

modestly covering their knees
and rolling their eyes

laughing over husbands and kids.
I laughed with them.

When the ladies in the neighborhood
moved away to bigger houses
and larger backyards,
I missed their conversations

about life I didn't yet understand
but looked forward to knowing.

The Water Fountain

No one notices at first.
But then they rarely do,
as she plods forward
with her two little dogs.

Count the steps, pass the mailbox.

Keep your straw hat on
the one with the navy trim,
even if the dogs are confused
when you wear it.

Heavy-soled boots practical when it
snows
worn every day now,
lift them one at a time
her steps less sure but persistent.

The sidewalk has cracks and
warning lines as she trudges ahead.

Once, there was a park around

the corner

with its water fountain

in the center.

Abruptly, she changes course.

It's still here.

Where fresh drops sprinkle the air.

Where she can take an errant breath,

once again.

Sea Grass

One day when the
air was soft

and the knowing of starfish and abalone
led her to pools of seawater,

she saw ripples of
current that had to be

listening as she tucked her feet in between crevices,
waiting for the magic to return.

Just then a hermit crab with a conch on its back,
started out, hesitating between stalks
of sea grass,
uncertain whether reproach awaited him

yet bold enough to travel
across boundaries,
marked by blue and violet algae

while drops of summer rain
left mist and memories on

orange and yellow lichen,
not yet nurtured by the
morning sun.

When Snow Walks In

Just sitting there.
Looking forward to a murky pancake
and syrup that stares back from a small
stainless pitcher—

when Snow walks in.

Long legs, suede brown coat, black straight
skirt with kick pleat. Cautiously,
she looks around.

I'd like to paint her but first
must get the sketch down as pencil beckons.

Ponytailed road runner waitress
scurries back and forth, then stops,
"Know what you want?"
I order.

Snow settles into a nearby booth. I apply

pencil to paper, wondering what the label

says on her skirt. Who is the designer?

Being short waisted, would her look be as good on me?

In a few minutes, the waitress slams the plate down.

She's had too much coffee.

I nudge the edge of the pencil.

Shade the curve of Snow's sleeve.

Salt the single egg, over easy, careful not to let it run into

the bacon.

Drip syrup across the pancake.

"Are you finished?" the ponytailed waitress asks, as she

scrutinizes my half-eaten breakfast.

I nod.

She drags my plate across the table.

It makes a cracking sound.

Sketching black satin sandals,
how does Snow balance on those heels?

Study the porcelain of her face. Shade the lips, nostrils,
dark brown hair with streaks of mandarin.
Can't hear what she orders.

The waitress slams the plate down in front of her.

I drag the lead around a ruffle.
Lace is hard to draw, it becomes a quick flourish.
What about the violet ribbon in her hair?
A moment of sketching brings her silhouette to life.

Snow plunks a few dollars down on the counter
and disappears.

Sand Dunes

Bill and I used to park below the sand dunes.
Strange lights would shoot out from the peak
of Mt. Blanca.
We wondered where they came from—
UFOs, no doubt.

A coyote sometimes crossed the road
in front of us, nodding toward the
headlights before ghosting away.

"What are you thinking?" he would ask.
"Nothing at the moment—*maybe*
why we're here."
"Don't you want to be here?"
"Not especially."

Those are the things I should have said.

Not speaking up cost me.
It always cost me.

Sand dunes are curious mounds of sand
driven through corridors of time collected
into mountains. Some like to ski straight down,
others use inner tubes to spin all the way to the bottom.

I never got the point. Skiing meant snow, lots of it.
But I didn't get the point of lots of things.
Like how I wanted to experience life but not be
hurt by it.

I wanted to be there, but not really.
Study it all from a safe distance away.
Not get in too deep, so I could back out
if I wanted to.

How could I know what I liked
if I didn't understand how it worked.

Sam and Rosalie

Five o'clock morning, Sam steers the dated 1971 de Ville
toward a trash can filled to the brim.

He hears the strains of Mozart's *Concerto in A Major,*
wafting from a nearby house.
He used to play that piece once.

That was a long time ago, when satin cummerbunds
mattered and rehearsals took full weeks.
Seldom was there time for hikes on rocky trails,
searching for fossils.

Don't get too close to the edge.

He pulls out spectator heels from the trash bin.
Should be worth twenty or so.
Places them on the front seat.

On a scrap of paper, he writes,
Houses fine as dust,
before the wind.

He knocks off the mud of a small Persian rug,
smooths the fibers back.
It might cover the lump in the floorboard
caused by the water leak, last summer.

Dogs run toward him, snarling.
"Nice doggies." He backs up,
dives into the car and slams the door.

They jump up, scratch the paint. He
drives away, laughs
turns down another street.

They track me down,
now surround me.
Teeth like death snares,
as morning tangles with the stars.

Rosalie limps over to the sink,
the fine spider cracks are getting larger.
She lifts the melamine cup to her lips,
sips, coffee stains still there, needs
another soaking.

She glances around at the wall clock,

brought back from another outing,

and at the velour screen covered with cupids and roses;

almost a Fragonard if you squint, needs some touching

up, amazing what others will throw away.

Rubs her aching knees, the arnica cream is

over on the shelf.

Checks the calendar.

He's not due back for a couple more days.

She pushes a tiny dish with her foot

toward the amber spotted feline.

Here, kitty.

Reaches for a *National Geographic*,

pages through geothermal Roman baths and Greek

pillars in Torcello churches.

The wind whips around the stucco.

Seems to come out of nowhere,

making rattling sounds she can't

always explain.

The radio is playing Bach's *Courante;*

reminds her of the cello she used to have,

maybe Sam will find another one for her. And a clarinet

for himself. Maybe even old sheet music.

They can reclaim echoes from the concert hall,

where they once played. She can still hear

the applause.

Kindness

Fifth Avenue rainstorm
surges through gutters,
churning soot colored water.

Wheelchair tips over
almost
passersby lift the old woman to safety.

Streetlight changes.
Jobber drags dolly across curb.
Bins containing precious cargo
slide forward,
almost dropping onto the wet street.

Good Samaritan scrambles
to restore his load.

Subway C uptown express,
mom and little girl
sell candy bars for a dollar each.

Passengers holding on to straps

search pockets for exact change.

After five stops,

mom and daughter exit quickly.

On Being Saved

When Aunt Zip was fifteen,
she embroidered rosebuds
on pillowcases,

carefully folded them
in her hope chest and waited.

At thirty, she embroidered
morning glories on place mats,

with matching napkins
and spun lace onto dresser scarves.

When she was forty-five, Aunt Zip
embroidered poems of sunshine

and the Lord's Prayer
on velvet cushions.

At sixty, she moved

to an island in the middle of the sea,

embroidered lions and tigers

on linen squares,

and waited.

Green Man

Captured by demons on that lonely road
now locked in a carving. His leafy
countenance transformed
into nature's stormy gaze.

I glance up at the lintel above the window
in the Yorkshire farmhouse.

Green Man stares back.

Friend of gargoyles and meadow elves,
warding off netherworld spirits.

By trade a cobbler, his shoes
sought by farmers and
tradesmen. Garrick was off
that afternoon to deliver boots on order.

Must return before dark.

She-Willow stood by the gate.

Garrick was late.

She would look for him in the woods.

All that remained was the horse and carriage.

I climb the ladder to reach the loft,

hoping for another sighting.

A cornet of honeysuckle gathered at her throat,

She-Willow appears above the steps.

Green Man sees her,

his face no longer a scowl.

The window is open a crack.

At midnight, Green Man and She-Willow

slip away into the forest.

My face reflects full moon's light.

I am transformed into She-Willow once again.

Lady Godiva

She rides through Coventry
without a stitch on.
A bet with her husband, the earl
to reduce taxes.

"The people will starve," she pleads.
The earl laughs, throws scraps to his dogs.

"Ride through the streets naked," he challenges.
She lets her gown fall, unclasps her rubies and soft pearls.
Blinds are drawn.
Only the noon sun, a witness.

Heralds lead the way.
Across bridges, past towers and gables,
her horse, dressed in gilded harness,
gallops on.

A successful ride,
taxes reduced,
the town showers her with field flowers.

What next?

A monastery to build,
land to give away.
Perhaps another ride,
another day.

Venice Beach

The homeless stare
hover wink at the rest of us,

as we return their gaze in our pink
and orange bikinis, on sale at the shop across
from the pickleball courts.

Watch out for the scooter that's dragging
the pit bull behind him.

Seagulls pick apart what's left of the sausage sandwich
embedded in a flimsy cardboard box.

Along the shoreline, butterfly shell clams
(we used to call them Donax) burrow
quickly beneath the surface just as the tide pulls away.

Frustrated sandpipers veer to the left.
A bleached sand dollar becomes unstable infrastructure.

Reaching into a basket of shells, I find a chunk of
transparent aquamarine. Reminds me of those
sea glass earrings I wear when I think of you. Wondering
where those pieces began their journey.

Possibly as close as a thrown away Coke bottle,
not romantic but relevant.
Chess players take note of such things.

Paris

Over-washed chalcedony sky,
canaries yellow in tender cages
under market tents,
trade songs with one another.

My elbows weary, search
for magazines *en anglais*
sold by *bouquinistes,*
along the Seine.

In Shakespeare and Company,
A Room of One's Own falls off the shelf.
I pick it up.

Inside a café, the glass water bottle violet, reflects
a woman, outside the window,
slouching under a noir jacket.

Couples dodging cloudbursts search for
metro carnets in their pockets.

Bicycles spin from place to place while
gargoyles sing from Notre Dame.

Long-necked chestnut trees border Les Halles.

Renoir prints are grabbed by tourists
hurrying down steps below Montmartre,
to collect children on the carousel,
flickering by.

Sarah Bernhardt and Alphonse Mucha

A smooth stone captures ink
guarding the image
Gismonda stands tall, amazon
draped in brocade.

Sarah is enchanted
by the artist and his lithographs.

Her career waning,
she must recapture the audience.

Posters are circulated everywhere.
They have divine properties.
From coffee houses in the Palais-Royal
to markets in the Marais.

In *La Dame aux Camelias*,
Sarah wears white satin draped
with ermine tails.

As she balances on aging floorboards,
the artist continues his lithographs nouveau.

Wearing white lilies in *La Plume*, her

hair is ringed by a blue halo and cache of stars.

Play after play, his posters mirror her elegance

driving the sorcery. Sarah is his muse.

Devoted to the whisper of her presence

Alphonse waits for her,

every gesture studied

as he wraps her in illustrated dreams.

THREE

Perfection

I can stand only
so much perfection.
Fresh raspberries in crème fraiche
must hurt my teeth.

The golf course grounds
bordered by
jasmine and orchid trees,
must have run-off that forms
a muddy trail.

Perfection is numbing.
There comes a time
when it all blends
together.

So it has to be raspy
and needling
and oxidizing

or else how can I feel

the sway of a broken
branch

snapped by the wind
or maybe worse.

The ball of string must
unravel
fingerprints must be
left on freshly painted steps.

The ceiling fan must buzz.
The zipper must get stuck, at
the bottom of my jacket.

The light in the study
must burn out.
The sea glass hard to find.

Chasing the Unicorn

The bus jaunts along Boulevard Saint-Germain
a block away from the Musee de Cluny,
a breath away from *The Lady and the Unicorn* tapestries.

The guard says (in French) the tapestries are not here
they are on tour,
sealing my fate.

They hang between old Roman baths
in thick-walled rooms,
or so I've been told.
Space is never wasted in Paris.

Five tapestries
five senses
the sixth connects man and wisdom.

The Unicorn falls prey to the Lady's
temptations or is it the other way
around?

Remind me to run my fingers through
his woolly hair.

They are poised so orderly,
remember I never got to see them,
so my imagination can run amuck.
Either way, too orderly for me.

Is that the first hint?
The Lady always in the center, the lion on her right,
the Unicorn on her left
a lamb, a dog, a monkey, a cat, symbols everywhere.

Is the Unicorn the dream and the lion reality or
is there much more to it than that?

My Unicorn runs up the canyon through the
Alpes de Provence. A white phantom wrapped in
the Le Viste coat of arms.

He is awake, no longer seduced
by the magic necklace the Lady stores in her jewel box.

The enchantment is over.

Embroidered are the mysterious words
Mon Seul Desir (My Soul's Desire).

The crimson roots of madder no longer
shielded by darkness.

Lost for 300 years
now lost to me.

The Lady chases the Unicorn to no avail
the handmaid is his love.

Without a word, she serves her mistress
and waits
her heart harbors true.

Testing Fate

Lying in bed
flannel sheets,
cozy
light still on.

A line steals across my mind
what was it.

Why didn't I remember to
have that pen and paper handy.

What was that scene, phrase, image?

If I get out of bed
I may lose that string of words forever.

Maybe it answered the letter he sent
maybe it was dialogue she needed to say
in a special way,
to him or to herself.

Please recapture it,

play it back so I can hear the

melody those words played.

Maybe I'll test fate and get up

to find that pen and paper

but is the risk too great

will the devil in the words

whisk them away forever?

Maybe I can get up so quietly

that my second self

won't realize I'm gone

and while this second self

listens for the footsteps of

that whispering phrase,

I can search for a working

pen and scrap of paper

to capture

that elusive thought once again.

In Edinburgh's National Gallery

Wandering through vermilion rooms
rewarded by van Goghs and Monets, to be sure

but on the teal wall straight ahead hangs the painting
that startles—Botticelli's *Simonetta Vespucci.*

Dear Sandro she was as beautiful as the legends
that called her *The Queen of Beauty,*

painted with undertones of terre verte and overtones
of rose petals and coral fire,
flaxen hair braided with pearls.

Are the whispers true that you were in love?

Every fine line and brushstroke reflected your
deliberate hand down to the intaglio
she wore around her neck.

Is that what gave you away?

She died at twenty-two.

You wanted to be buried next to her,

unrequited love, they said.

Years later, she was immortalized

in *The Birth of Venus*.

Translucent skin with alabaster powder.

Aphrodite at sea in mirrors of light.

Simonetta haunted your finest work.

How did you remember every detail of

her countenance?

Now you are both united in the

Church of Ognissanti.

The gallery is closing, everyone has gone.

All that remains is the intaglio,

clutched in my hand.

Crosstown Muse

You came to me while riding the bus
driving me to write then and there

but I didn't know how to begin.

You opened the door.

Every jarring movement
compelled new words
opened spaces
closed doubts
introduced me to my heroine.

Down Wilshire we flew
she had red hair
a riveting stare.

Her energy pushed me through corridor after corridor.
I couldn't write the words down fast enough.

Crossing Fairfax,
Vermont.

At Westmoreland, she taxed me with her fervor
pushing me on, building a firestorm.

Crossing Figueroa
then Flower,
Alameda train tracks.

Don't be afraid to stumble
one wild horse to another.

The Sibyls of Siena

Trapped in the Duomo by day
Delphi and the rest of the Sibyls
(composed of white marble)
have plenty to say about
salvation and resurrection

while they read Virgil at night
by the light of the Cathedral lantern.

Memories of Mt. Olympus pervade when
guided by rainstorms and whirlwinds,
the Sibyls pronounced wisdom upon heraldic gods
and the mortals who slept with them.

Now they share their knowing with women wilted,
holding toddlers by the hand while

lighting novena candles, searching for bathrooms
along the way.

Delphi holds her burning torch above Sphynx.
"Let's go to the races today. We'll cover
ourselves in mist so no one sees us."

"What about the scrolls?" Sphynx asks. "They are
too heavy to carry."

"Leave them with Cumana and the cherubs.
You are a winged cat. Take a stretch
or two from time to time while I find a
a rose to waft through my hair. Virtue has
deserted me."

"Do you know the way?" Sphynx asks.

"We'll follow the street where shops
are stocked with lavender
and pottery stores sell faces of the sun and the moon.
We'll pass doorways where photographs
of mamma and papa hang side by side and wallpaper
curls up in the corners."

Sky Window

When Betty told me about the great kiva
not far from town,
I begged to see it.
Did kivas really exist?

I rushed out from the car,
scrambled up the wall,
lowered myself
down the wooden ladder,
through the narrow square of light
to the packed earth floor below.

Swept into the underworld,
where moccasins had danced
and geometric symbols covered walls,
explaining dimensions and universes I
knew little about.

The power was all around me
I was on special ground,
not knowing how to access it.

Wondered if my grandfather
(who was part Indian) would have
participated in such ceremonies.

If I listened hard enough
would the songs handed down by my ancestors
be sung to me,
about how the world was born and
the people who had come from the stars?

If I dreamed close enough to the earth beneath my feet
with the sky window above,
would my dreams be big enough
to carry rainbows and lightning spears across the river?

And if I looked hard enough, would I see my brothers
sitting shoulder to shoulder
nodding in smoky trance,
listening to storytellers whose visions came from their
breath and from the great chiefs before them.

The Light Under the Doorway

It's just bright enough for me to see
tomorrow hidden behind that kitchen
chair.

And the Fiesta plates stacked
even the one that got broken (how did that happen?)

So sure I had dried them carefully.
Where is the music coming from?
Strolling one-note at a time across the tiled
linoleum.

Someone has turned it off.
That means I'm not alone.
Hello? Is that you?

Keep the window open. It lets the hot air out.

That goes for anyone who's out there.

Do you like the yellow curtains?

Still not sure they were the right length.

But then 45 inches seemed long enough

at the time.

Possibly the mail lady.

But she hasn't come by, yet.

The dog has stopped barking.

He usually warns me.

Usually.

Swap Meet

She pulls up in the converted school bus,
looking for *her* spot.
The grandkids, all five of them, pile out
and help her set up.
"Put the blue glass ashtray
and Christmas decorations here.
That painting of the woman walking in the desert,
over there."

She knows that woman in the painting, thought about
her on and off. Maybe will go for twenty-five,
even with the paint flaking off in the corner.
Hopefully, to someone who appreciates it.

The couple next to her plays Jimmy Reed's *Shame,*

Know you got me baby,
up against this fence
and that's a shame, shame,
shame, on you.

Cranking it up all the way, until daylight
is squeezed between eleven and two o'clock,

when the rugs and banjo,

might as well be packed up again.

She arranges the Bobbsey Twins books.

They can be sold as a set, so the stories

will stay together.

The jewelry case has war medals and key chains.

Separated at first, then piled up on top of

each other. The Kewpie doll has lost her wig.

She pulls out the sandwiches, peanut butter and jelly, and

passes them around.

"Who wants one?"

Teri's dress has a tear in it.

Sassy is thirsty. "There's a water fountain down in front

of the grandstand,

come right back."

That lace tablecloth has a spot on it.

Was it there before?

"I'll read you a story tonight, when we get home."

Summer's Lament

Every day she sits on the stoop waiting
for the paper boy

for anyone to break the monotony
of a stalwart summer

bringing death to flies too lazy to move
out of the reach of the swatter.

A humid day good for dressing up
in mother's gown and amethysts

navigating down the long staircase
it feels like flying
the dress catches on the heel of her
shoe

she slips
recovers barely.

Hang onto the banister,

don't fall

even though it was summer's ennui

that drove her to this madness.

When are we going to the beach?

Hands already sinking into the sand, feeling for

sand dollars and unbroken shells,

Dad takes forever to get ready.

The Tam O'Shanter green-plaid

thermos with the yellow lid

holds one gallon of iced tea,

enough for the four of us and

hot dogs we can grill over tired ashes.

Where are the matches and when are

we leaving?

Lodestone

Lodestone is magnetite,
a piece of iron ore.
Magnetized to charm.

Is that what happened to me?

Hurtling through on a starry night.
Searching for a glow, a light inside the window,
settling on me.

An impossible connection at first glance
but there it is, ignoring the off-chance
that it was meant for someone else

and I just got in the way.

Persistent foghorns.
The clock at the Embarcadero
struck midnight,

warning everyone there was magic in the air

leading to a casual stroll,

up the winding road to Coit Tower

where my purse was stolen.

So unexpected that night,

but so was everything else.

The Plane Trip

I pack my suitcase
then it's easy to say,
I can't turn back now.

Maybe the plane trip will be rough,
maybe I'll meet a fair-haired boy
who sits next to me.

Maybe he'll ask, what do you do?
I'm a poet, I'll answer
but don't ask me to show
you a poem.

Or maybe if I had taken the
seat on the other side of the plane,
would there still be a fair-haired
boy to ask, what do you do?

And if so, I would say, I write songs and
play the piano
and he would say play for me, sometime.

I would have to say I only

play with one hand,

and he would say, how come?

That's all I've ever learned, I'd say.

I don't tell him if I played with both hands

he might insist I play for him and he might be

disappointed because he's heard better,

but I won't care because I decided

not to sit on that side, anyway.

Maybe I won't take the plane trip after all,

the taxi will only drive me

around the block before I say,

I forgot something and have to go home.

He drops me off

I go back inside and unpack.

I am safe.

Weight

What if she lost that last
ten pounds?

Suppose the perfect model
look no longer haunted her.

The clothes, hung so
beautifully
she could always lose the weight.

Suppose she could pass on the
cookie that winks and
choose the cottage cheese instead
and never lusted for size zeros

what if she wished to please only herself,

and her mirror said she was perfect and disciplined.

There were no shadows playing on her mind.

There was great self-respect,
she received approval from everyone.

Rabbit brush and cactus
never scratched her
when she ventured too close
to the side of the road.
If only …

Mom's Photo

Young and pretty,
she is in color.
An atmosphere of clouds all around.

Mother stares at me,
she has seen into the future
and knows I will
leave her.

She demands that I stand by her,
take care of her at all costs.

I am a little girl again
reaching for her hand,
marching off to the
dentist. No comfort here.

Where is the little girl that lives inside her,
who was marched to the
dentist by her mother. Unyielding.

Can I be friends with her?
Who posed her in a world of
lights and darks.
She must become her own beacon,
color must be nourished.

The relatives surrounding her live in straight spaces,
never leaving their photographs,
all together in a plastic box
under the bed,

except for Mother's sepia tone in its silver frame,
up on the shelf, behind me.

CPSIA information can be obtained
at www.ICGtesting.com
Printed in the USA
BVHW072212251120
594189BV00011B/494/J